Carter

Please!

Don't
touch
My
Book

# mommy
# & me
# bake

# DK

## LONDON, NEW YORK, MUNICH, MELBOURNE, DELHI

Project editor  Laura Palosuo
Senior designer  Hannah Moore
US editor  Margaret Parrish
Photographer  Will Heap
Home economist  Denise Smart
Illustrator  Helen Dodsworth
Senior producer (pre-production)  Tony Phipps
Producer  Stephanie McConnell
Jacket designer  Claire Patane
Creative technical support  Sonia Charbonnier
Managing editor  Penny Smith
Managing art editor  Marianne Markham
Art director  Jane Bull
Publisher  Mary Ling

First American Edition, 2015
Published in the United States by DK Publishing
345 Hudson Street, New York, New York 10014

15 16 17 18 19   10 9 8 7 6 5 4 3 2 1
001-192950-02/15

A catalog record for this book is
available from the Library of Congress.
ISBN: 978-1-4654-2896-7

Printed and bound in China by Hung Hing.

Discover more at
**www.dk.com**

# Contents

 This symbol tells you that this is a "find out more" page.
These pages give you additional baking facts.

# Baking basics

Baking is lots of fun and with this *book* you will learn to make all kinds of yummy treats. To make sure you stay safe in the kitchen, here are a few important rules. Always be careful and follow the instructions.

## Kitchen rules

• When you're in the kitchen, you should ask an adult to move items in and out of the oven and to heat things on the stovetop.
• Ask an adult to help if you need to use a sharp knife or an electrical appliance.
• Wash your hands before and after you work with food. Always wash your hands after handling raw eggs and raw meat.
• Do not lick your fingers after you've worked with food.
• Check the use-by date on all ingredients.
• Follow the instructions on the packaging when storing food.
• The dessert recipes are meant as a special treat, so eat them as part of a balanced diet.

## Getting started

1. Read the instructions all the way through *before* you begin.
2. Gather together everything you need.
3. Have a cloth handy to clean up spills.
4. Put on an apron, tie back your hair, and wash your hands.

## Safety

All the projects in this *book* are to be made under adult supervision. When you *see* the warning triangle, be extra careful because hot stoves, electrical appliances, and sharp implements are used in making a recipe. Ask an adult to help you.

## Key to symbols

| Prep time | Cook time | Yield |
|---|---|---|
| How long it will take to prepare | How long it will take to bake in the oven | How many pieces or servings it will make |

Clean hands

# Basic baking gear

Here's equipment that's often used in baking. You'll need to use some of these items to make the recipes in this book.

Flour shaker

Sieve

Paper liners

Parchment paper

Cake pans

Rolling pin

Muffin pan

Spoons

Pastry brush

Baking sheet

Electric mixer

Cooling rack

Pastry cutters

Apron

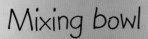
Mixing bowl

# find out more

# Weighing and measuring

Baking is chemistry in the kitchen. You need to get the amounts just right for the recipes to work as planned. There are many different ways to measure ingredients.

**Measuring spoons** are used for measuring small amounts accurately.

**Measuring cups** are used to measure dry ingredients.

Use a knife to level the cup to make sure you measure the right amount.

tsp = teaspoon      tbsp = tablespoon

Cups

¼ tsp

½ tsp

1 tsp

½ tbsp

1 tbsp

# US measures

oz = ounce, lb = pound
There are 16 ounces in a pound.

# Metric measures

g = gram, kg = kilogram
There are 1,000 grams in a kilogram.

## Measuring around the world

Different countries use different systems for measuring. Recipe ingredients are measured using either the **US** or the **metric** system. It doesn't matter which system you use—just make sure you don't mix up the systems within one recipe.

A **kitchen scale** can also be used to measure dry ingredients. Scales often indicate both US and metric units.

**Liquid measuring cups** are used to measure liquids. For an accurate measurement, make sure your eyes are level with the surface of the liquid.

Measuring cups show US and metric amounts

ml   fl oz
500          16

300           8

100

# US measures

fl oz = fluid ounce

# Metric measures

ml = milliliter
There are 1,000 milliliters in a liter.

find out more

# Ingredient magic

Like magic, ordinary sugar, eggs, butter, and flour turn into cookies in the oven. But did you know they all do different jobs? Here's what they each bring to the mix.

## Sugar

Everyone knows that sugar adds sweetness, but it also makes cookies browner and crunchier by caramelizing and absorbing moisture.

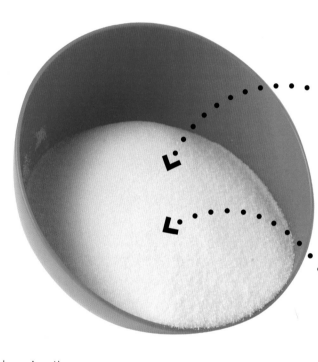

Makes cookies turn brown

Makes cookies crunchy

## Eggs

Eggs help cookies rise. They also give them structure because the liquid in eggs bonds with the flour and sets in the oven.

Helps cookies rise

Gives cookies structure

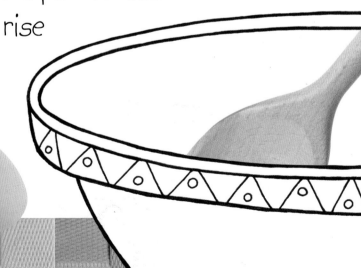

Adds flavor
to cookies

Helps make
cookies
crumbly

# Butter

Butter coats some of the flour in fat
and protects it from the liquid in a
recipe. This makes cookies crumbly.
Butter also adds flavor to cookies.

# Flour

The amount of flour in a recipe
makes cookies crumbly or chewy.
When the proportion of flour is
high, cookies are crumblier. Less
flour means chewier cookies.

Makes cookies
chewy or crumbly,
depending on amount

## Why do cookies spread?

In the heat of the oven, the butter
and sugar in cookies melt. This helps the
ball of cookie dough spread out flat.

after baking

before baking

the ball of dough
has spread out flat

9

# Crunchy cutout cookies

This simple cookie dough is quick and easy to make, leaving you plenty of time for the fun part—rolling it flat and cutting out shapes.

Cut out all your favorite golden. This recipe make.

Dragonfly

## You will need

16 tbsp butter, cut into cubes

²⁄₃ cup superfine sugar

1 large egg yolk

1 teaspoon vanilla extract

2 cups all-purpose flour

...shapes and bake them until
...hough to share with friends.

Butterfly

### Iced cookies
These crunchy cookies are delicious eaten just as they are, but you can also decorate them. Turn to pages 14–15 for colorful icing ideas.

# Equipment
• Mixing bowl • Wooden spoon
• Sieve • Plastic wrap
• Rolling pin • Cookie cutters
• Baking sheet • Palette knife
• Wire cooling rack

1 hour
to make
(including 30
minutes
chilling)

8–10
minutes
to bake

makes
30
cookies
(depending
on cutters)

# Making cookie dough

Follow the steps to make the dough for your cookies. It's as easy as 1, 2, 3, 4!

beat it

**1** Beat the butter and sugar together in a bowl until the mixture is light and fluffy and changes color slightly.

stir it

**2** Add the egg yolk and vanilla extract and stir them in. Next, sift in the flour and mix again to make a dough.

squeeze it

**3** Using your hands, bring the dough together and mold it into a ball. If pieces fall off just stick them on again until you have a solid ball.

wrap it up

**4** Wrap your dough in plastic wrap. Put it in the fridge and let it chill for 30 minutes before you start making your cookies.

# Making crunchy cutout cookies

roll it flat

**1** Preheat the oven to 350°F (180°C) Dust your work surface with flour and roll out the dough to about ¼in (½cm) thick.

cut out shapes

**2** Use cookie cutters to cut out your cookies. Gather the trimmings into a ball and roll it out again to make more cookies.

**3** Move the cookie shapes onto a nonstick baking sheet. Bake them for 8–10 minutes, then place on a rack to cool.

# Icing cookies

Mix up some icing and add colorful sprinkles to turn your cookies into delicious works of art.

 +  +  =

³/₄ cup
confectioners' sugar

3 tsp water

A few drops of
food coloring

Colored icing

1 Add water to the sugar a little at a time and stir well. Add the food coloring.

2 Use a small spoon to spread the icing over the top. Add sprinkles and let the icing harden.

Use writing icing to add details and decoration.

Make a few blossoms or a whole meadowful.

## Equipment

- Butter knife • Plastic wrap
- Rolling pin • Baking sheet
- Wire cooling rack

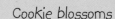

# Cookie blossoms

If these flowers look good enough to eat, it's because they are! You can make your swirly blossoms any color you like by using different shades of food coloring.

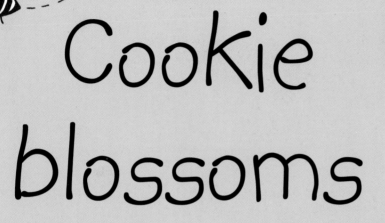

## You will need

Basic cookie dough (see p. 12)

A few drops of food coloring

1 tbsp cocoa powder

15 minutes to make (plus 15–30 minutes chilling)

12–14 minutes to bake

makes 26 cookies

# Making blossom cookies

These steps show you how to make chocolate swirls and pink swirls, but you can create any color combination you like by adding the colors you want in step 2.

divide it ⚠️

wrap it up

**1** Heat the oven to 350°F (180°C). Divide the dough into four equal pieces and shape each piece into a ball.

**2** Add a few drops of food coloring to one ball of dough and work it in. Knead the cocoa powder into another ball.

**3** If the dough feels soft after mixing in the colors, wrap it in plastic wrap and chill it in the fridge for 15–30 minutes.

roll the dough

**4** Take a colored ball of dough and roll it out into a rectangle. Roll out one of the plain balls to the same size.

**5** Lay the plain-colored rectangle on top of the colored one, trimming off any excess. Roll the rectangles together lengthwise, as shown.

slice it

**6** Using a blunt knife, cut disks about 1/4in (1/2cm) thick from the roll. Then repeat steps 4-6 with the other two balls of dough.

**7** Spread the cookies onto a nonstick baking sheet and bake them for 12-14 minutes, then place on a wire rack to cool.

## Go big!

Make giant swirly blossoms by rolling up all four balls of dough. Cut the dough into disks and bake as above.

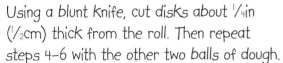

Cookie machine

## You will need

7 tbsp
butter, cubed

1 large
egg

²/₃ cup
superfine sugar

¹/₂ tsp
vanilla extract

1¹/₄ cups
self-rising flour

# Cookie factory

Turn your kitchen into your very own cookie factory and make lots of different kinds of cookies with this simple recipe. Then watch the orders come flooding in!

| 40 minutes to make (including 30 minutes chilling) | 15 minutes to bake | makes 16 cookies |
|---|---|---|

## Equipment

• Large mixing bowl • Electric mixer or hand whisk • Wooden spoon • Sieve • 2 baking sheets • Parchment paper • Wire cooling rack

Box them up and send them to friends.

# Making cookies

Make the dough first, then add your toppings. You can mix and match them to make as many kinds of cookie as you like.

*whirr!*

**1** Preheat the oven to 350°F (180°C). Beat the butter and egg together using an electric mixer or hand whisk until light and fluffy.

**2** Stir in the sugar and vanilla extract using a wooden spoon. Add the flour, sifting it in a little at a time.

**3** Work the flour into the mixture with a wooden spoon until it forms a soft dough. Cover the bowl and put it in the fridge to chill for 30 minutes.

*shape*

**4** Use your hands to shape the chilled dough into 16 balls. Space them out evenly on baking sheets lined with parchment paper.

You can make different kinds of cookie at the same time— just vary the toppings.

decorate

**5** Flatten the balls gently with your hand and press the toppings into the cookie dough. Bake in the oven for 15 minutes, then transfer to a wire rack to cool.

Your cookies will spread out flat as they bake so be sure to leave plenty of space between them.

# Making chocolate cookies

It's easy to turn your plain cookies into chocolate ones. Just mix two teaspoons of cocoa powder into the flour before you add it to the cookie dough in step 2.

Plain chocolate

Double chocolate and marshmallow

# find out more What happens in the oven?

Cake batter goes in, and, as if by magic, fluffy cake comes out. It's actually heat and a little chemistry that turn ingredients into cake.

Mmmm

⚠ Ovens are **HOT!** Be careful near ovens and always ask an adult to move items in and out.

### Don't open the door!

If you do, the cake may not rise correctly, and it may even shrink! Heat helps the cake rise by making the bubbles in the batter bigger. Opening the door will lower the temperature in the oven and the bubbles will get smaller and the cake may sink. Never open the door until three-fourths of the baking time has passed.

Oven mitts

*smells good!*

## Preheating the oven

By heating the oven first you make sure that the temperature is right before the cake goes in.

# How it works

When you make cake batter, you cream butter and sugar together, which creates lots of little air bubbles. When egg and flour are added they surround these bubbles. In the heat of the oven, the bubbles get bigger and the cake batter rises around them. When it gets hot enough, the egg and flour set (turn solid) and hold everything in place.

Small air bubbles

Big air bubbles

Watch the cake rise through the window

For a good result, set a timer.

### Is it done?

Use a skewer, a toothpick, or even a strand of dried spaghetti to test your cake. The cake is ready when the tester comes out clean.

These cupcakes are...

# Cupcake heaven

easy to make an

Soft, springy, light as air—
you might just float away in delight
when you bite into one of these
otherworldly creations.

## You will need

³/₄ cup sugar

11 tbsp
butter, cubed

3 eggs

1 tsp vanilla
extract

1¼ cups
self-rising flour

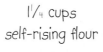

## Equipment

• Mixing bowl • Electric mixer
• Small bowl • Fork • Sieve • Spatula
• 2 muffin pans • 20 paper liners
• Spoon • Wire cooling rack

30
minutes
to make

15
minutes
to bake

makes
20
cupcakes

o yummy you'll keep coming

back for more.

### Frosted delights

These cupcakes are delicious eaten just as they are, but you can also frost them. Turn to pages 30–33 for frosting recipes and ideas.

The tops of the cupcakes rise into high peaks.

# Making cake batter

It's important to cream the butter and sugar and beat the eggs well to get lots of air into the mixture. This will help your cakes rise.

whisk the eggs

1 Cream the sugar and butter together in a bowl until light and fluffy.

2 In a separate bowl, whisk the eggs and vanilla extract with a fork.

3 Pour in the egg mixture and combine it with the butter and sugar.

sift the flour

fold the mixture

4 Sift the flour into the bowl. You can tap the sieve with your hand to help the flour through.

5 Use a spatula to fold everything together. Do this carefully so you don't flatten the bubbles.

# Making cupcakes

1 Preheat the oven to 350°F (180°C).
Line two muffin pans with 20 paper liners.

2 Use a spoon to divide the cake batter between the liners.

frost the cupcakes once they're cool

3 Bake in the oven for 15 minutes, until golden and just firm.
Cool in the pans for 5 minutes, then place on a cooling rack.

# Frosting cupcakes

## Confectioners' sugar

Cut out a template and sift confectioners' sugar over the top for a sweet, simple decoration.

1 tbsp confectioners' sugar

⭐1 Using scissors, carefully cut out a template from parchment paper.

⭐2 Hold the template in place and sift the confectioners' sugar over the top.

## Cream cheese

Use cream cheese to make a thick and creamy frosting without any butter.

 ³/₄ cup cream cheese  +  2 tbsp confectioners' sugar

⭐1 Put the cream cheese and sugar into a medium-sized mixing bowl.

⭐2 Mix them together until you have a creamy, spreadable frosting.

# Chocolate ganache

This rich frosting uses dark chocolate.
For a sweeter taste, add sugar.

 8oz (225g)
dark
chocolate **+**  1 cup
heavy
cream

**1** Put the chocolate in a heatproof bowl.
Bring the cream to a boil. As soon as it
is at a boil, pour it over the chocolate.

**2** Stir until the chocolate has melted and
is fully mixed in. Set aside for 5 minutes.
Blend until the ganache holds its shape.

# Buttercream

Beat butter and sugar together to
make a smooth, creamy frosting.

 6 tbsp
butter, cubed **+**  1½ cups
confectioners' sugar **+**  A few drops
food coloring

**1** Sift the confectioners' sugar over the
butter. Use a wooden spoon to mix it in.

**2** Add food coloring and 1–2 tsp water
and beat the mixture until it's fluffy.

# Decorating cupcakes

Frost the cupcakes. Then add sprinkles, candies, or fruit to make original cupcake creations.

Combine frosting and sprinkles for a classic look.

frosting colors

Who-who

butterfly cake

Cut the top off the cupcake and cut the top in half. Spread on frosting and arrange the halves as wings.

marshmallow sheep

Use ganache or writing
icing to add details

*sprinkle*
## sprinkle
# sprinkle

spreading

Start in the middle of the
cupcake and spread the frosting
with the back of a spoon.

candies

### Cupcake art

It's time to let your imagination
run wild! Turn your cupcakes
into animals, monsters, or
bugs—or make beautiful little
cakes fit for a princess. Look
on this page for ideas and then
design your own cupcakes.

# pretzel butterfly

# Spotted cake

Go wild and make a cake that's spotted
like a leopard or striped like a tiger. Then
stand back from the feeding frenzy.

## You will need

Basic cake batter
(see p. 28)

2 tbsp cocoa
powder

## Equipment

- Parchment paper • Scissors
- 7in (18cm) round baking pan
- Tablespoon • Small sieve
- Butter knife

# Making spotted cake

The spots in this cake are actually chocolate cake! The chocolate cake is made by adding cocoa powder to regular cake batter. We do it in the same bowl so clean-up is a snap.

1 Preheat the oven to 350°F (180°C). Cut out a circle of parchment paper to fit your pan, then grease the pan and line it.

2 Drop spoonfuls of the batter into the pan, making sure you leave gaps between them. Stop when you've used up half the mixture.

3 Add the cocoa to the remaining mixture using a small sieve. If you end up with clumps in the sieve, break them up with the back of a spoon.

4 Mix the cocoa powder into the batter with a spoon until it's smooth and glossy. This will make the spots or stripes in your cake.

**5** Drop spoonfuls of the chocolate batter into the gaps. Use a big spoon to make big spots or a smaller spoon for smaller spots.

**6** To make stripes, drag a knife through the spots. Bake the cake for 30 minutes, or until a wooden toothpick comes out clean.

Once cooked, turn the cake onto a rack and let it cool before cutting it into 8–10 slices. Each slice will have a different jungle pattern.

# Pineapple upside-down cake

This topsy-turvy cake is made the wrong way around. You start with the top and finish with the bottom.

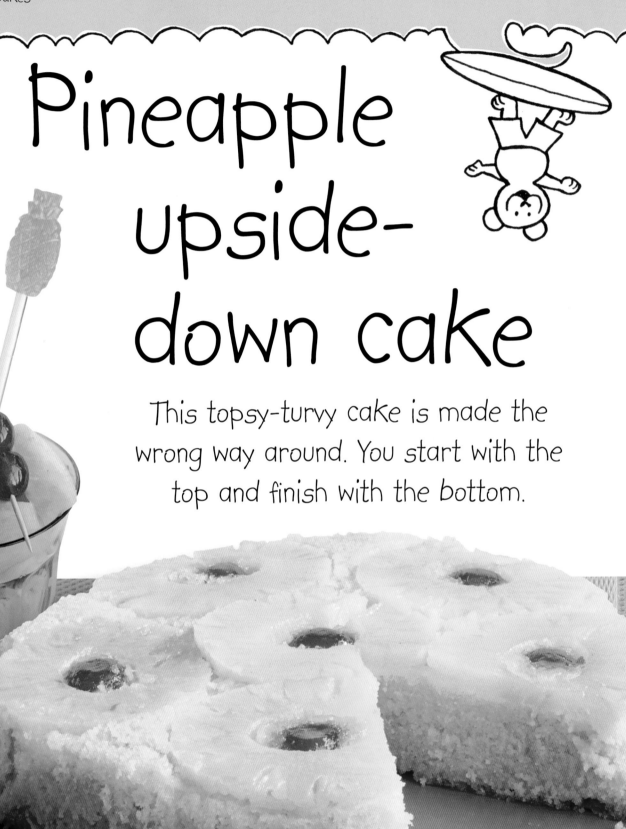

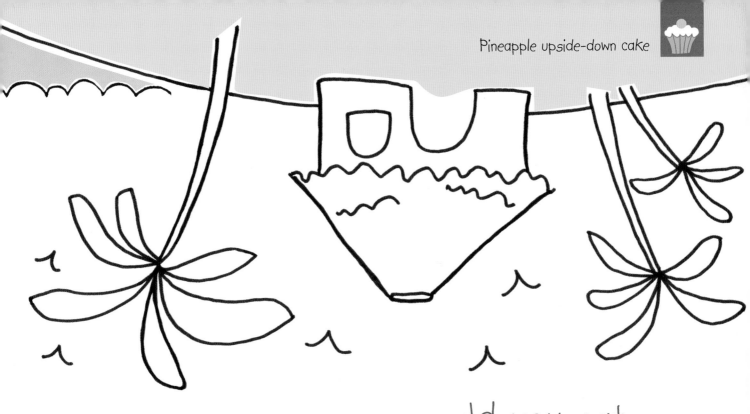

In an upside-down world, would you eat right-side-up cake?

| 10 minutes to make | 25-30 minutes to bake | makes 8 servings |

## You will need

Basic cake batter
(see p.28)

7 pineapple rings

7 maraschino cherries

## Equipment

• 8in (20cm) cake pan with removable bottom
• Parchment paper
• Large spoon • Serving plate

39

# Making the upside-down cake

This surprising cake makes a yummy dessert or a tropical treat for a party. It's especially delicious with ice cream.

grease the pan

add the pineapple

**1** Heat the oven to 375°F (190°C). Grease the inside of your pan with *butter*, using a piece of parchment paper to spread the butter.

**2** Arrange the pineapple rings on the bottom of the greased pan. If they don't fit without overlapping, you can trim them a bit.

# Turning the cake upside down

turn the cake over

**1** When *baked*, ask an adult to take the cake out of the oven and let it cool slightly. Then cover it with a plate that's larger than the pan.

**2** Ask an adult wearing oven mitts to slide one hand under the cake and put another hand on top and then turn the cake in one quick movement.

3 Put cherries into the centers of the pineapple rings. Make sure their bottoms point down— that's what you'll see when you flip the cake.

cover the fruit

4 Carefully spread the cake batter over the fruit and smooth it out with a large spoon. Bake the cake for 25–30 minutes, until golden on top.

3 Carefully remove the outer ring of the cake pan. It may help to jiggle the ring slightly to loosen it before lifting.

ta-da!

4 Lift off the removable bottom for the big reveal. Ta-da! You can eat the cake warm or wait for it to cool before serving it.

# A tower of brownies

Chewy on the outside and gooey on the inside, these brownie blocks are just about perfect.

## You will need

18 tbsp butter, cut into cubes

10oz (275g) dark chocolate (70% cocoa)

1¼ cups superfine sugar

3 large eggs

1 tsp vanilla extract

1⅓ cups all-purpose flour

2½oz (75g) white chocolate chunks

## Equipment

- Saucepan • Wooden spoon
- Large mixing bowl
- Electric mixer or hand whisk
- 9in (23cm) square cake pan
- Parchment paper
- Cooling rack

20 minutes to make

20–25 minutes to bake

makes 36 squares

# Making brownies

You'll have lots of fun stirring up this gooey, glossy brownie mixture. Keep a close eye on your brownies as they bake—they should be slightly fudgey in the middle.

I like extra chocolate chunks in my brownies.

melt chocolate

**1** Heat the oven to 350°F (180°C). Melt the butter and chocolate over low heat, stirring occasionally. Let cool slightly.

**2** Using an electric mixer or hand whisk, cream together the sugar, eggs, and vanilla extract until the mixture is fluffy and light in color.

pour in chocolate

**3** Pour the chocolate and butter into the egg and sugar mixture bit by bit. Mix everything together with the electric mixer or hand whisk.

**4** Add a little flour and stir it into the mixture with a wooden spoon. Keep adding and stirring until all the flour is combined.

sprinkle in the white chocolate chunks

**Stir-in substitutes**

If you don't like white chocolate, you can add chocolate chips, nuts, or raisins instead.

5 Pour in the white chocolate chunks and fold them into the mixture until they are evenly spread throughout.

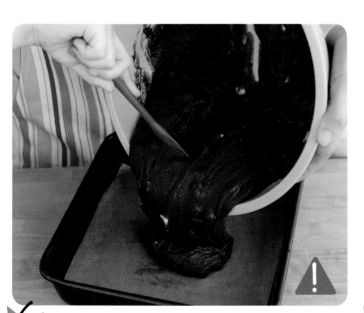

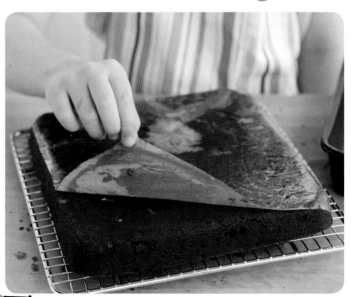

6 Spread the mixture into a lined pan. Bake on the center rack for 20–25 minutes, until the brownies are just set and a bit gooey in the middle.

7 Let the brownies cool for 10 minutes in the pan. Then turn onto a cooling rack. When cool, remove the parchment paper and cut into squares.

# Why does dough rise?

Water and flour make a stretchy dough to trap the gas bubbles that yeast produces. This makes the dough rise.

## Why do we need to knead?

Kneading makes the dough elastic. When it's really stretchy, it can hold the gas bubbles that the yeast makes. As more and more bubbles are made, the dough will start to rise.

1 Knead the dough with the heel of your hand.

2 Pull the dough, then fold it in half.

3 Turn the dough and knead again.

## On the rise

Letting the dough rise is called **proofing**. This is usually done in a warm place. It lets the yeast get to work before the dough is baked.

at the start of proofing

### What is yeast?

It's a live fungus! Dried yeast is inactive until warm water is added, then it begins to feed on sugars in the bread flour. It releases bubbles as part of the feeding process, causing the dough to rise.

## Push

Push the dough away from you to stretch it.

## Pull

Pull it toward you to stretch it before turning.

Catch as many bubbles as you can in your dough.

The dough continues to trap *bubbles* and has risen high up in the bowl.

after 30 minutes

after an hour

big bubbles

tiny bubbles

# Tear-and-share bread

The best thing since sliced bread, this homemade loaf is made for sharing. Bring it out to "oohs" and "aahs" from friends.

pumpkin seeds

poppy seeds

sesame seeds

sunflower seeds

## You will need

3½ cups bread flour

¼oz (7g) package fast-acting (instant) dried yeast

1 tsp salt

1 tsp sugar

1–1¼ cups tepid water

Milk for brushing

## Equipment

- Large mixing bowl • Large spoon
- Dish towel • 9in (23cm) baking pan
- Pastry brush • Wire cooling rack

Tear-and-share bread

20 minutes to make (plus 90 minutes rising)

30 minutes to bake

makes 7 large rolls

49

# Making basic bread dough

Making your own bread is easier than you might think.
You can use this recipe to make whole wheat bread, too—
just replace the white bread flour with whole wheat flour.

pour

combine

**1** In a large mixing bowl, combine the flour, salt, sugar, and fast-acting (instant) yeast. Make a well in the center and pour in the water.

**2** Use a spoon and, once the dough becomes too sticky, damp hands to combine all the ingredients together into a ball.

knead

cover

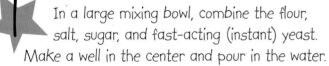

**3** Sprinkle some flour onto the work surface. Turn out the dough and knead it for 10 minutes, pushing it, stretching it, and folding it until smooth.

**4** Put the dough back in the bowl. Cover the bowl with a damp dish towel and leave it in a warm place for an hour, or until the dough has doubled in size.

**5** Once it has risen "punch down" the dough by punching it lightly in the middle. Then knead it lightly on a floured surface. It's now ready to use.

# Making tear-and-share bread

**Smooth moves**
Make rolls that are smooth and plump by tucking the sides under, stretching out the top as you do.

*shape into rolls*

*sprinkle*
*sprinkle*
*sprinkle*

1  Preheat the oven to 425°F (220°C). Divide the dough into seven equal-sized pieces, or as many as will fit in your pan. Then shape each piece into a round roll.

*brush*

2  Grease the pan with butter and place the rolls snugly inside. Cover the pan with a damp dish towel and let it rise for 30 minutes more.

3  Using a pastry brush, brush the tops of the rolls with milk.

4  Sprinkle the seeds you like on top. Bake the rolls for about 30 minutes, until golden. Move to a wire rack to cool.

Bread

# You will need

Basic bread dough
(*see* p. 50)

Pasta sauce or
tomato purée

Green bell pepper   Olives

Mushrooms        Corn

Pepperoni        Basil

Onions      Mozzarella
cheese

# Equipment

• Rolling pin • Tablespoon
• Cutting board
• Knife • 2 baking sheets

pizza people

15 minutes to make

10-15 minutes to bake

makes 4 pizzas

and pizza pets

woof, Woof!

# Making pizza people and pets

Making pizza faces is easy and so much fun. What will yours look like?
It could be a happy person, a silly person—even someone you know.

roll the dough

spread the sauce

**1** Preheat the oven to 425°F (220°C). Split the dough into four balls. On a floured surface, roll each ball into a round pizza crust.

**2** Move the crusts onto baking sheets. Spread one large tablespoon of sauce on each one. You can use jarred sauce or tomato purée.

# Pizza inspiration

mushroom ears and olive eyes

Woof, woof!

broccoli hair and onion glasses

sprinkle cheese

make a face

**3** Sprinkle grated mozzarella all over the sauce-covered crust. Do the same on the other three pizzas.

**4** Make a face on your pizza with your chosen toppings. Bake for 10–15 minutes, until the dough is crisp and the toppings are cooked.

Add salad hair after your pizza is cooked.

Squeak, squeak!

baby corn nose and bacon eyebrows

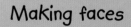

### Making faces
You can use lots of different ingredients to make a pizza face— look on this page for ideas.

# Breadsticks

You can also use the bread dough to make crunchy, cheesy breadsticks.

These breadsticks make great party or picnic food. You can also make plain ones—they're perfect for dipping.

## You will need

Basic bread dough (see p. 50)

½ cup grated cheddar cheese

15 minutes to make

10-12 minutes to bake

makes 36 breadsticks

## Equipment

- Rolling pin
- Pizza cutter or knife
- Baking sheet

⚠ roll out the dough

⭐1 Heat the oven to 425°F (220°C). Turn the bread dough onto a floured surface and roll it into a long rectangle.

cut the dough ⚠

⭐2 Using a pizza cutter or a knife and starting at the short edge, cut the dough into strips that are roughly ³/₄in (1cm) wide.

roll the strips

⭐3 Roll each strip under your hands so that it's round all over and transfer to a baking sheet.

sprinkle ⚠

⭐4 Sprinkle with cheese and bake for 10-12 minutes. Let cool before eating.

# Bouncy bread

Jump right in and make this springy Italian-style bread with basil and tomatoes. It's tasty with soups and salads.

## You will need

Basic bread dough
(see p. 50)

A handful of
basil leaves

10 cherry
tomatoes

¼ cup
olive oil

## Equipment

• Rolling pin
• Baking sheet
• Cutting board
• Knife

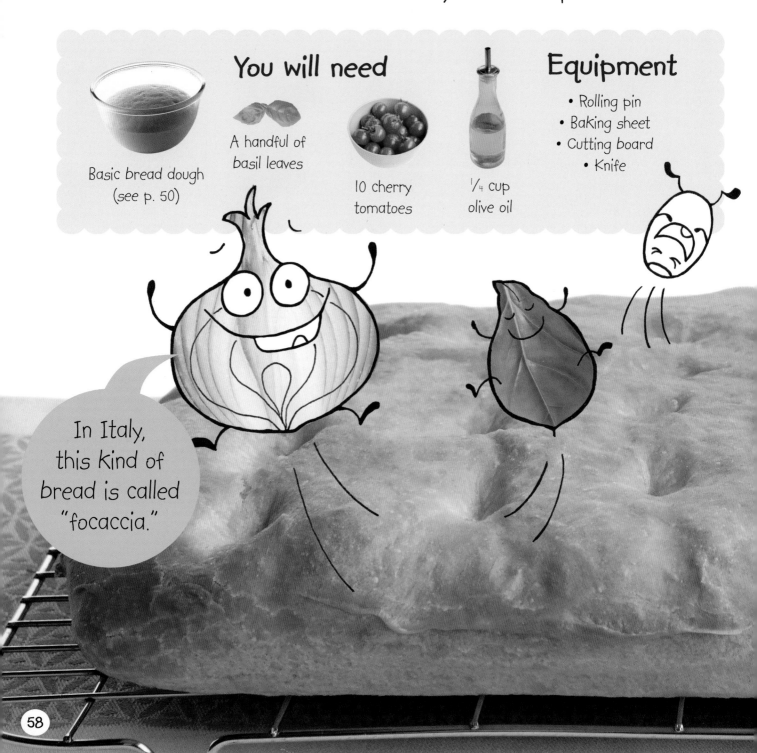

In Italy,
this kind of
bread is called
"focaccia."

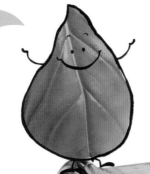

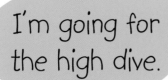
I'm going for the high dive.

Olive oil

## Topped or not?

This bouncy bread is yummy plain, but you can add all kinds of toppings—tomatoes, olives, onion, even potatoes—for an even tastier treat. Turn the page for tasty topping ideas.

10 minutes to make (plus 30 minutes rising)

25 minutes to bake

makes 9 portions

# Making bouncy bread

You can recognize this bread by its dimples. You make them with your finger.
They help the bread rise evenly and provide a place for the olive oil to collect.

roll

**1** Heat the oven to 425°F (220°C). Roll the dough into a rectangle to fit your baking sheet.

stretch

**2** Lift the dough into an oiled baking sheet, stretching it to fit. Cover it with a dish towel and let it rise for 30 minutes.

poke

**3** Next, poke some holes into the dough with your finger. You can also use the handle of a wooden spoon.

# Topping ideas

Tomato and basil

Potato and rosemary

decorate

drizzle

⭐4 Now add your toppings. Cut the tomatoes in half and press them into the dough. Press in *basil* leaves between the tomatoes.

⭐5 Drizzle the bread with olive oil, sprinkle some salt on top, and bake it in the oven for about 25 minutes, until the surface is golden brown.

Black olives

Red onion

**Top this!**
It's easy to make all these different kinds of bread. Just add the raw toppings in step 4. They will cook as the bread bakes.

pastry cutters

# What makes pastry crumbly?

The best pastry is light, crumbly, and melts in your mouth. To make it, you'll need flour, butter, and a little know-how.

**Rubbing in** Start by rubbing the butter into the flour. This coats the flour in fat and stops the dough from becoming stretchy.

**Resting** Handling pastry too much can make it hard. This is why the dough needs to rest after you've made it.

### Chef's tip
"Keep yourself and your pastry cool" is the advice given to pastry chefs. This is because heat from your hands can melt the butter in pastry, making it soggy. Keep your pastry cool by chilling it in the fridge and by working quickly so it doesn't have time to warm up.

keeping cool

flour shaker

**All floured up**
Even chilled pastry can stick to the table. Make rolling easier by dusting flour on your hands, the rolling pin, and your work surface. Pastry that doesn't stick is also easier to work with.

rolling pin

cooked pastry is crumbly

**Rolling out** Roll your pastry out quickly and confidently so you don't overwork it.

# Queen of

The queen of tarts she made jam tarts, all on a summer's day...

# jam tarts

Make jam tarts fit for a King
or queen with this simple recipe
that uses only four ingredients.

## You will need

| 2 cups all-purpose flour | 7 tbsp butter | 3 tbsp water | Strawberry jam |

## Equipment

• Large mixing bowl • Tablespoon
• Plastic wrap • Rolling pin • Round pastry
cutter • Muffin pan • Small cookie cutters
• Wire cooling rack

30 minutes to make (plus 30 minutes chilling)

15 minutes to bake

makes 24 tarts

# Making basic pastry

Making pastry is easier than you might think, but there are a few rules to follow to ensure that it turns out as planned. Don't overwork your pastry and remember to let it rest in the fridge.

rubbing in

**1** Put the butter and flour into a bowl. Use your fingers to rub them together until the mixture looks like bread crumbs.

pouring

**2** Add three tablespoons of water to the mixture a little at a time. You can measure it all into a measuring cup first if you like.

**3** Bring the mixture together into a ball using your hands, but be careful not to overwork it. The sides of the bowl should now be clean.

wrap and chill

**4** Wrap your pastry in plastic wrap and chill it in the fridge for half an hour, or until firm.

# Making jam tarts

rolling

cutting

**1** Preheat the oven to 400°F (200°C). Roll out the pastry to 1/8in (4mm) thick.

**2** Cut circles with a pastry cutter. Save the scraps to cut shapes for the top.

**3** Press the pastry circles into the muffin pan. The edges should stick out a bit.

filling

**4** Spoon jam into the pastry crusts until they are half full. Use small cookie cutters to cut out shapes for the tops from the pastry scraps.

**5** Place the pastry shapes on top of the jam. Bake in the oven for about 15 minutes, then transfer to a wire rack to cool.

35
minutes
to make

15–20
minutes
to bake

makes
12
tarts

# Veggie wheels

These savory tarts are perfect for eating on the go.
Take them on a picnic or put them in a lunchbox.

## You will need

Basic pastry
(see p.66)

³/₄ cup
corn

4¹/₂oz (125g)
red bell pepper,
diced

4¹/₂oz (125g)
broccoli

¹/₄ cup
grated cheese

2 large eggs

## Equipment

- Rolling pin • Pastry cutter
- 2¹/₂in (6cm) round tart pans
- Cutting board • Knife
- Measuring cup
- Fork • Baking sheet

¹/₂ cup
cream

¹/₂ cup
milk

# Making veggie wheels

Once you know how to make pastry, you'll make these wheels in no time at all. You can eat them warm out of the oven, but they are also tasty cold.

rolling out

**1** Preheat the oven to 400°F (200°C). Roll out the pastry to 1/8in (4mm).

**2** Cut circles from the pastry with the pastry cutter. You can also use a cup.

**3** Lay each pastry circle over a pan. Press it into place so that it fits the pan.

filling

**4** Use your hands or a knife to separate the broccoli "trees" from the stem. This makes them easier to fit into the veggie wheels.

**5** Fill the pastry crusts three-quarters full with corn, peppers, and broccoli. Move the pans to a baking sheet.

*whisking*

6 Whisk the eggs together with the milk and cream until evenly combined.

*pouring*

7 Pour the mixture into the crusts and sprinkle cheese on top. Bake for 15–20 minutes, until the filling sets, and let cool before serving.

### Ham and cheese wheels

Make these tarts in the same way as the veggie wheels. Just add some chopped cooked ham in Step 5.

# Fruit boats

Treats ahoy! Serve these amazing fruit-filled boats as a delicious dessert or after-school treat.

**Fruit flotilla**

We have used boat-shaped tart pans to make these boats, but you can use round ones, too.

## Equipment

• Rolling pin • Boat-shaped tart pans • Parchment paper • Baking beans or dried beans • Mixing bowl • Wooden spoon • Cutting board • Knife

20 minutes to make

13 minutes to bake

makes 16 tarts

## You will need

Basic pastry (see p. 66)

5¹/₂oz (150g) mascarpone cheese

2 tbsp confectioners' sugar

¹/₂ tsp vanilla extract

 Blackberries

 Peaches

 Blueberries

 Strawberries

 Kiwis

 Raspberries

# Making fruit boats

These pastry shells are baked without any filling.
This is called "baking blind." We fill them with special baking beans
to help them keep their shape, but you can use dried beans instead.

**1** Roll out the pastry and cut it into rectangles that are bigger than the pans. Lay a rectangle of pastry over each pan and press it in.

**2** Roll a rolling pin across the top of each pan to cut off the edges. Preheat the oven to 400°F (200°C).

**3** Cut a piece of parchment paper to fit each boat. Fill them with *beans* and *bake* for 10 minutes. Remove the *beans* and paper and *bake* for 3 minutes more.

mixing

cutting

**4** Allow the pastry shells to cool before taking them out of their cases with the help of a knife. In a bowl, mix the cheese, sugar, and vanilla together until smooth.

**5** Wash the berries and fruit that you're using. Cut the bigger fruit into shapes that will fit your pastry boats. Make sure you cut a few tall shapes to use as sails.

Watch out—here come pie-rates!

6 Fill the cooled pastry shells with the cheese mixture and position the fruit on top. Treats ahoy!

# Chicken turnovers

These chicken and potato turnovers contain a mini-meal in a little pastry. They are perfect for buffets and picnics.

## You will need

Basic pastry
(see p. 66)

2oz (50g) potato

2oz (50g)
sweet potato

4oz (115g) cooked
chicken (1 breast)

115g (40g)
cream cheese

2 scallions, chopped
1 tbsp chopped parsley

1 egg,
beaten

## Equipment

• Cutting board • Knife • Mixing bowl • Wooden
spoon • Rolling pin • 4½in (11cm) pastry cutter • Fork
• Pastry brush • Baking sheet • Wire cooling rack

### Pasties

You can also make bigger turnovers, called pasties, perfect for lunch on the go. Use a small plate to cut out bigger pastry circles and prepare as directed.

20 minutes to make

25-30 minutes to bake

makes 6-8 turnovers

Cheep, cheep!

# Making chicken turnovers

These turnovers are made with cooked chicken but raw vegetables.
In the oven, the vegetables cook in the cream cheese sauce. Yum!

**1** Preheat the oven to 400°F (200°C). Chop the potato, sweet potato, and chicken into ½in (1cm) cubes.

**2** Mix together the cream cheese, scallions, and parsley. Add the other ingredients to the bowl.

stir

**3** Stir all the ingredients together, making sure that everything is evenly coated in the cream cheese mixture.

cut out

**4** Roll out the pastry. Cut out circles using a round pastry cutter.

spoon filling

**5** Put a large spoonful of filling into the middle of each pastry circle.

brush

**6** Use a pastry brush to brush egg along one half of each pastry circle.

fold
press
stick

**Crimping**
To close your turnovers tightly, squeeze the dough together with your fingers all along each edge.

7 Fold over the pastry circles. Use your fingers to crimp the edges. Pierce the tops a few times with a fork.

8 Move the turnovers to a baking sheet and brush them with egg. Bake them in the oven for 25–30 minutes, then cool on a rack.

Each turnover contains a tasty meal.

# Index

*Now it's time to clean up and do the dishes.*

## Acknowledgments

**With thanks to:** Wendy Horobin and Anne Hildyard for additional editing and James Mitchem for proofreading.

**With special thanks to the models:** Abi Arnold, Emily Fox, Olive Hole, Cassius Moore Cockrell, Eleanor Moore-Smith, Kaylan Patel, Edward Phillips, Dylan Tannazi, Isabella Thompson.